D1121515

Published 2008 by Concordia Publishing House
3558 S. Jefferson Avenue, St. Louis, MO 63118-3968
1-800-325-3040 • www.cph.org

Illustrations © 2008 by Concordia Publishing House
Verses 1 and 2, written by unknown; Verse 3 written by
John Thomas McFarland (1851-1913)

All rights reserved. No part of this publication may be reproduced, stored
in a retrieval system, or transmitted, in any form or by any means, electronic,
mechanical, photocopying, recording, or otherwise, without the prior written
permission of Concordia Publishing House.

Manufactured in China.

1 2 3 4 5 6 7 8 9 10   17 16 15 14 13 12 11 10 09 08

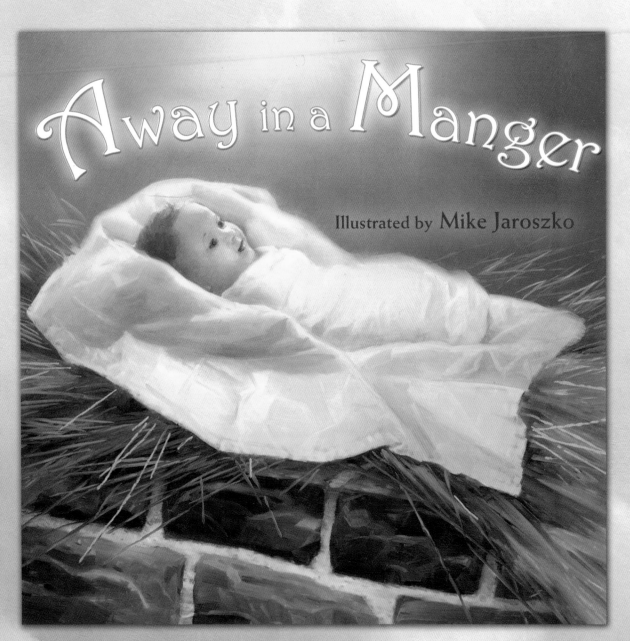

Away in a Manger

Illustrated by Mike Jaroszko

CONCORDIA PUBLISHING HOUSE • SAINT LOUIS

Away in a manger,
No crib for a bed,

The little Lord Jesus
Laid down His sweet head.

The stars in the sky
Looked down where He lay,

The little Lord Jesus
Asleep on the hay.

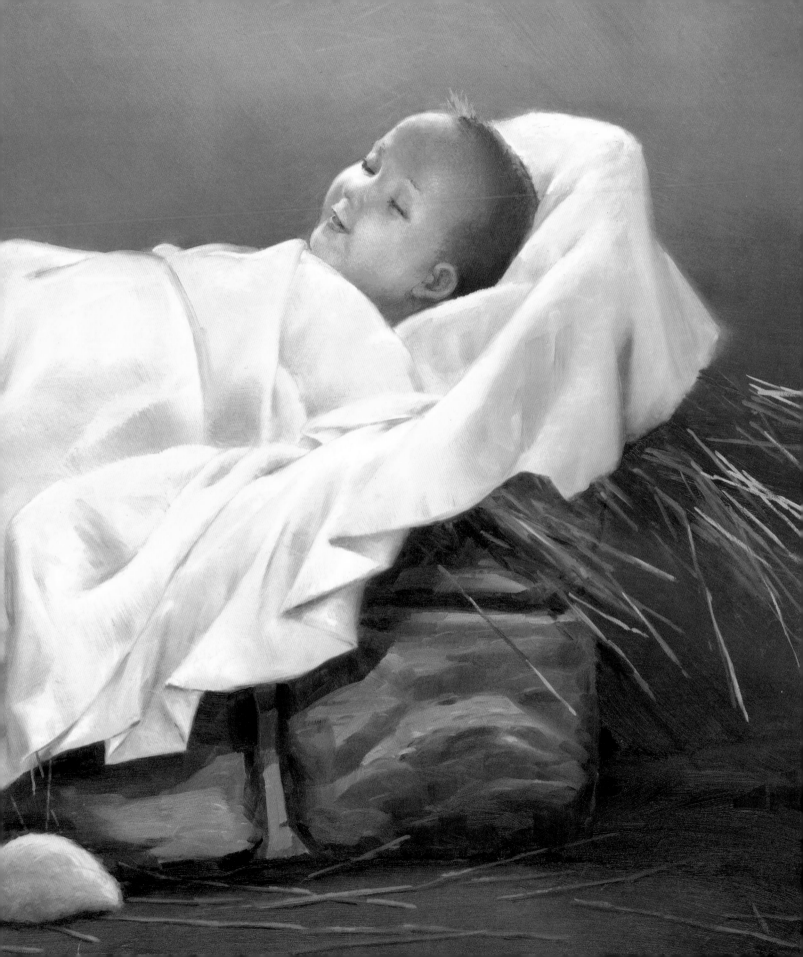

The cattle are lowing,
The baby awakes,

But little Lord Jesus,
No crying He makes.

I love Thee, Lord Jesus!
Look down from the sky,

And stay by my cradle
Till morning is nigh.

Be near me, Lord Jesus;
I ask Thee to stay

Close by me forever
And love me, I pray.

Bless all the dear children

In Thy tender care,

And take us to heaven

To live with Thee there.